What Is a Plant?

 HOUGHTON MIFFLIN HARCOURT

PHOTOGRAPHY CREDITS: (c) ©Corbis; 3 (b) © Tony Fagan/Alamy; 4 (t) ©luca gargano/Flickr Open/Getty Images; 4 (b) Michael P Gadomski/Getty Images; 6 (b) ©Comstock Images/Jupiterimages/Getty Images; 8 (t) ©Tony Hertz/ AgStock Images/Corbis; 9 (b) ©Ross M Horowitz/Stone/Getty Images; 10 (bl) ©Richard Griffin/Alamy Images; 11 (tl) AgStock Images/Corbis; 11 (tr) ©Todd Muskopf/Alamy Images

Printed in China

ISBN: 978-0-544-07227-5

14 15 16 17 0940 20 19 18 17

4500693646   A B C D E F G

Be an Active Reader!

 Look at these words.

seed	stem	flower	cone
root	leaf	fruit	

 Look for answers to these questions.

How are plants different from animals?

What are seeds and roots?

What plant parts can we see?

How does a plant use its parts?

How are flowers different from cones?

How are young plants and their parents alike and different?

What are some ways we sort plants?

How are plants different from animals?

Animals can not make their own food. They eat plants or other animals. Plants make their own food.

Many animals can walk and run. Other animals can swim or fly. Plants can not move from place to place on their own.

This rabbit can not make food.

What are seeds and roots?

A seed coat protects a seed.

A new plant has sprouted.

Many new plants grow from seeds. A seed is the part of a plant that new plants grow from. Seeds grow in soil. Suppose you put soil in a cup. Next, you put seeds in the soil. Then, you put the cup in a sunny place. You water it, too. What do you think will happen next?

What happens to a plant below the ground? Plants have roots. A root grows down into the soil. Roots hold the plant in place. Roots take in water from the soil. They take in nutrients, too. Nutrients are things in soil that help plants grow. All plants need water and nutrients to live.

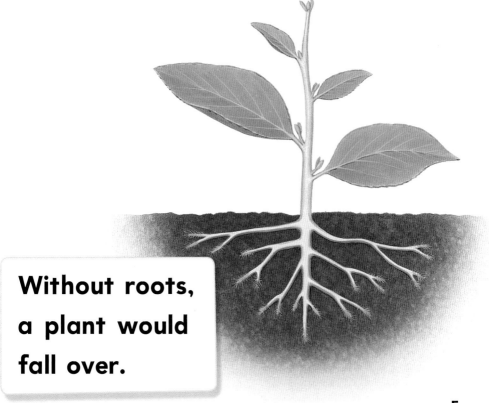

Without roots, a plant would fall over.

What plant parts can we see?

Plants have stems. A stem holds the plant up. Stems move water and nutrients to all the parts of a plant. A leaf is the part that makes food for the plant. It uses light, air, and water. A flower is the plant part that makes seeds. Seeds can grow into new plants.

flower

leaf

stem

How does a plant use its parts?

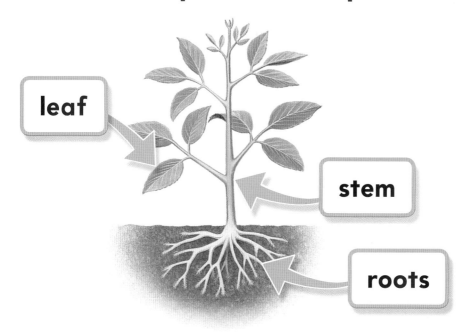

The plant uses its parts to make food. First, the roots carry water and nutrients to the stem. The stem carries water and nutrients to the green leaves. The leaves take in sunlight and air.

The leaves use sunlight, air, water, and nutrients. They make food for the plant.

How are flowers different from cones?

orange tree with flowers

Some trees have flowers. Other trees have cones. Fruit trees grow flowers. Deep inside the flower are parts that can form fruit. A fruit is the part of the plant that holds seeds. The fruits cover and protect the seeds inside. Fruit seeds can grow new fruit trees.

Some trees have cones. The cone is the part of a non-flowering plant that holds the plant's seeds. When the cone opens, seeds fall to the ground. These seeds can grow new trees.

A pine tree has cones.

How are young plants and their parents alike and different?

Some adult plants have flowers and fruits. They have different leaf shapes, too. Young plants are similar to their parents. Their leaf shape can be similar to their parents' leaf shape. Young plants are smaller.

The young tomato plant has no tomato yet.

Apples come from trees.

This maple was green.

What are some ways we sort plants?

We eat some plants. We can eat apples from an apple tree.

We can sort plants by their leaves, too. Some trees have green leaves all year round. Other trees have leaves that turn different colors. The leaves fall to the ground.

Be a Scientist

Bring a hand lens outside. Look at some plants. Ask yourself: Do I see seeds, roots, and stems? Does this plant have flowers or cones? Are the leaves big or small? Are they thin or wide? Make a list of what you see.

 Write About Plants

Cut out magazine pictures of plants. Glue each picture on an index card. Write a caption for each. For example: I can eat the fruit on this plant. Discuss with a friend.